SCHOLASTIC
READ & RESPOND

Bringing the best books to life in the classroom

Activities based on Charlotte's Web
By E.B. White

Recommended system requirements:
Windows: XP (Service Pack 3), Vista (Service Pack 2), Windows 7 or Windows 8 with 2.33GHz processor
Mac: OS 10.6 to 10.8 with Intel Core™ Duo processor
1GB RAM (recommended)
1024 x 768 Screen resolution
CD-ROM drive (24x speed recommended)
Adobe Reader (version 9 recommended for Mac users)
Broadband internet connections (for installation and updates)

For all technical support queries (including no CD drive), please phone Scholastic Customer Services on 0845 6039091.

Eynsham Community Primary School

Designed using Adobe Indesign
Published by Scholastic Ltd,
Book End, Range Road, Witney,
Oxfordshire OX29 0YD
www.scholastic.co.uk

Printed and bound by Ashford Colour Press
© 2015 Scholastic Ltd
1 2 3 4 5 6 7 8 9   5 6 7 8 9 0 1 2 3 4

British Library Cataloguing-in-Publication Data A catalogue record for this book is available from the British Library.
ISBN 978 1407 14223 4

Due to the nature of the web, we cannot guarantee the content or links of any site mentioned. We strongly recommend that teachers check websites before using them in the classroom.

Authors Debbie Ridgard and Sally Burt
Editorial team Rachel Morgan, Jenny Wilcox, Red Door Media, Marion Archer
Series designer Neil Salt
Design team Ian Foulis and Mike Connor
Illustrator Gemma Hastilow
Digital development Hannah Barnett, Phil Crothers and MWA Technologies Private Ltd

Acknowledgements
The publishers gratefully acknowledge permission to reproduce the following copyright material:
ICM Partners for the use of extracts from *Charlotte's Web* by E.B. White. Text © 1952, E.B. White. (1952, Hamish Hamilton). **Penguin Group UK** for the use of text from *The Diary of a Young Girl* by Anne Frank, edited by Otto H. Frank and Mirjam Pressler, translated by Susan Massotty. Text © 1991, The Anne Frank–Fonds, Basle, Switzerland. (English translation © 1995, Doubleday, a division of Bantam Doubleday Dell Publishing Group Inc. (1997, Viking). **Penguin Group UK** for the use of text from *Zlata's Diary* by Zlata Filipovic, translated by Robert Laffont. Text © 1993, Zlata Filipovic. (1994, Penguin Books) **Curtis Brown Group Ltd** for the digital use of text from *The Secret Diary of Adrian Mole Aged 13 3/4* by Sue Townsend. Text © 1982, Sue Townsend. (1982, Methuen) **Penguin Group UK** for the print use of text from *The Secret Diary of Adrian Mole Aged 13 3/4* by Sue Townsend. Text © 1982, Sue Townsend. (1982, Methuen) **Penguin Group UK** for extracts and illustrations from *Diary of a Wimpy Kid* by Jeff Kinney. Text and illustrations © 2007, Jeff Kinney (2007, Harry N. Abrams; 2008, Puffin Books) **Penguin Group UK** for the use of the cover from *Charlotte's Web* by E.B. White, illustrated by Garth Williams. Text © 1952, J white (1952, Hamish Hamilton).

Every effort has been made to trace copyright holders for the works reproduced in this book, and the publishers apologise for any inadvertent omissions.

CONTENTS ▼

INTRODUCTION

Read & Respond provides teaching ideas related to a specific children's book. The series focuses on best-loved books and brings you ways to use them to engage your class and enthuse them about reading.

The book is divided into different sections:

- **About the book and author:** gives you some background information about the book and the author.

- **Guided reading:** breaks the book down into sections and gives notes for using it with guided reading groups. A bookmark has been provided on page 8 containing comprehension questions. The children can be directed to refer to these as they read.

- **Shared reading:** provides extracts from the children's books with associated notes for focused work. There is also one non-fiction extract that relates to the children's book.

- **Grammar, punctuation & spelling:** provides word-level work related to the children's book so you can teach grammar, punctuation and spelling in context.

- **Plot, character & setting:** contains activity ideas focussed on the plot, characters and the setting of the story.

- **Talk about it:** has speaking and listening activities related to the children's book. These activities may be based directly on the children's book or be broadly based on the themes and concepts of the story.

- **Get writing:** provides writing activities related to the children's book. These activities may be based directly on the children's book or be broadly based on the themes and concepts of the story.

- **Assessment:** short activities that will help you assess whether the children have understood concepts and curriculum objectives. They are designed to be informal activities to feed into your planning.

The activities follow the same format:

- **Objective:** the objective for the lesson. It will be based upon a curriculum objective, but will often be more specific to the focus being covered.

- **What you need:** a list of resources you need to teach the lesson, including digital resources (printable pages, interactive activities and media resources, see page 5).

- **What to do:** the activity notes.

- **Differentiation:** this is provided where specific and useful differentiation advice can be given to support and/or extend the learning in the activity. Differentiation by providing additional adult support has not been included as this will be at a teacher's discretion based upon specific children's needs and ability, as well as the availability of support.

The activities are numbered for reference within each section and should move through the text sequentially– so you can use them while you are reading the book. Once you have read the book, most of the activities can be used in any order you wish.

Below are brief guidance notes for using the CD-ROM. For more detailed information, please click on the '?' button in the top right-hand corner of the screen.

The program contains the following:
- The extract pages from the book.
- All of the photocopiable pages from the book.
- Additional printable pages.
- Interactive on-screen activities.
- Media resources.

Getting started

Put the CD-ROM into your CD-ROM drive. If you do not have a CD-ROM drive, phone Scholastic Customer Services on 0845 6039091.

- For Windows users, the install wizard should autorun, if it fails to do so then navigate to your CD-ROM drive. Then follow the installation process.
- For Mac users, copy the disk image file to your hard drive. After it has finished copying double click it to mount the disk image. Navigate to the mounted disk image and run the installer. After installation the disk image can be unmounted and the DMG can be deleted from the hard drive.
- To install on a network, please see the ReadMe file located on the CD-ROM (navigate to your drive).

To complete the installation of the program you need to open the program and click 'Update' in the pop-up. Please note – this CD-ROM is web-enabled and the content will be downloaded from the internet to your hard-drive to populate the CD-ROM with the relevant resources. This only needs to be done on first use, after this you will be able to use the CD-ROM without an internet connection. If at any point any content is updated, you will receive another pop-up upon start up when there is an internet connection.

Main menu

The main menu is the first screen that appears. Here you can access: terms and conditions, registration links, how to use the CD-ROM and credits. To access a specific book click on the relevant button (NB only titles installed will be available). You can filter by the

drop-down lists if you wish. You can search all resources by clicking 'Search' in the bottom left-hand corner. You can also login and access favourites that you have bookmarked.

Resources

By clicking on a book on the main menu, you are taken to the resources for that title. The resources are: Media, Interactives, Extracts and Printables. Select the category and then launch a resource by clicking the play button.

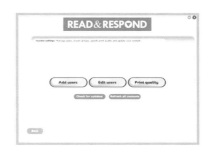

Teacher settings

In the top right-hand corner of the screen is a small 'T' icon. This is the teacher settings area. It is password protected, the password is: login. This area will allow you to choose the print quality settings for interactive activities ('Default' or 'Best') and also allow you to check for updates to the program or re-download all content to the disk via Refresh all content. It is from here that you can set up user logins so that you can save and access favourites. Once a user is set up, they can enter by clicking the login link underneath the 'T' and '?' buttons.

Search

You can access an all resources search by clicking the search button on the bottom-left of the main menu. You can search for activities by type (using the drop-down filter) or by keyword by typing into the box. You can then assign resources to your favourites area or launch them directly from the search area.

CURRICULUM LINKS

Section	Activity	Curriculum objectives
Guided reading		Comprehension: To maintain positive attitudes to reading and understanding.
Shared reading	1	Comprehension: To discuss and evaluate how authors use language, including figurative language, considering the impact on the reader.
	2	Comprehension: To draw inferences such as inferring characters' feelings, thoughts and motives from their actions, and justifying inferences with evidence.
	3	Comprehension: To check that the book makes sense to them, discussing their understanding and exploring the meaning of words in context.
	4	Comprehension: To provide reasoned justifications for their views.
Grammar, punctuation & spelling	1	Composition: To link ideas across paragraphs using adverbials of time (for example, 'later'), place (for example, 'nearby') and number (for example, 'secondly').
	2	Transcription: To use further prefixes and suffixes and understand the guidance for adding them.
	3	Composition: To use semicolons, colons or dashes to mark boundaries between independent clauses.
	4	Composition: To use modal verbs or adverbs to indicate degrees of possibility.
	5	Composition: To punctuate bullet points consistently.
	6	Composition: To recognise vocabulary and structures that are appropriate for formal speech and writing.
Plot, character & setting	1	Composition: To consider how authors have developed characters and settings.
	2	Comprehension: To draw inferences such as inferring characters' feelings, thoughts and motives from their actions, and justifying inferences with evidence.
	3	Composition: To identify the audience for and purpose of the writing, selecting the appropriate form.
	4	Comprehension: To understand what they read.
	5	Comprehension: To summarise the main ideas drawn from more than one paragraph.
	6	Comprehension: To distinguish between statements of fact and opinion.
	7	Comprehension: To summarise the main ideas drawn from more than one paragraph.
	8	Comprehension: To ask questions to improve their understanding.

Section	Activity	Curriculum objectives
Talk about it	1	Spoken language: To give well-structured descriptions, explanations and narratives for different purposes.
	2	Spoken language: To participate in role play.
	3	Spoken language: To articulate and justify answers, arguments and opinions.
	4	Spoken language: To use spoken language to develop understanding.
	5	Spoken language: To gain, maintain and monitor the interest of the listener(s).
	6	Spoken language: To participate in presentations and performances.
Get writing	1	Composition: To use further organisational and presentational devices to structure text and guide the reader.
	2	Composition: To describe settings, characters and atmosphere and integrate dialogue to convey character and advance the action.
	3	Composition: To identify the audience for and purpose of the writing, selecting the appropriate form.
	4	Composition: To select appropriate grammar and vocabulary, understanding how such choices can change and enhance meaning.
	5	Comprehension: To summarise the main ideas drawn from more than one paragraph.
	6	Composition: To identify the audience for and purpose of the writing, selecting the appropriate form and using other similar writing as models for their own.
Assessment	1	Comprehension: To understand what they read.
	2	Composition: To use commas to clarify meaning or avoid ambiguity in writing.
	3	Comprehension: To explain and discuss their understanding of what they have read, including through formal presentations and debates, maintaining a focus on the topic and using notes where necessary.
	4	Composition: To identify the audience for and purpose of the writing, selecting the appropriate form and using other similar writing as models for their own.
	5	Composition: To use further organisational and presentational devices to structure text and to guide the reader.
	6	Composition: To perform their own compositions, using appropriate intonation, volume, and movement so that meaning is clear.

CHARLOTTE'S WEB

About the book

Many people have described *Charlotte's Web* as their best-loved children's book of all time. Written by EB White and illustrated by Garth Williams, the story of Charlotte, the indomitable and resourceful spider, and her friendship with Wilbur, the runt of a litter of piglets saved by the farmer's daughter Fern, has endured for over half a century. It is a timeless story of friendship, loyalty and sacrifice made accessible by the animal characters. Set against a farmyard backdrop, with its inevitable cycle of life, children meet an unforgettable barnyard of characters – geese, sheep, cows and, of course, Templeton, the self-serving rat and reluctant anti-hero – who band together to help Charlotte outwit Mr Zuckerman, the farmer, and save Wilbur from becoming the Christmas ham. Like all good fables, the animals have a thing or two to teach humans.

In 1973, *Charlotte's Web* was made into an animated movie musical. Some 33 years later, in 2006, it was released as a full-length film, featuring real animals (except for Charlotte).

About the author

Elwyn Brooks White, better known as E.B. White, was born in 1899. During his career as a writer, he wrote more than 17 books of prose and poetry. In 1971, he won the National Medal for Literature and in 1973 he was elected to the American Academy of Arts and Letters. Despite having a career in writing, White reputedly claimed to find it 'difficult and bad for one's disposition'.

In 1938, the author moved to a farm in Maine and began writing children's fiction, initially to entertain his 6-year-old niece. *Stuart Little* was published in 1945 (also illustrated by Garth Williams), followed by *Charlotte's Web* in 1952 and *The Trumpet of the Swan*, his third and final children's novel, in 1970. He died on 1 October 1985, survived by his son and three grandchildren.

E.B. White often claimed to be more at home with animals rather than people: 'I like animals, and my barn is a very pleasant place to be, at all hours.' When asked if his stories were real, in an open letter to his young fans, White replied, 'No, they are imaginary tales… But real life is only one kind of life – there is also the life of the imagination.'

About the illustrator

Garth Williams, born in New York City to English artists in 1912, initially studied architecture before deciding to become an artist like his parents. He illustrated many classic children's books as well as *Charlotte's Web*, particularly the Little House books by Laura Ingalls Wilder. In 1951 he illustrated *Charlotte's Web*, using pen and ink, with his eldest daughter as his model for Fern Arable. He believed books greatly influence children and so used his illustrations to try to 'awaken something of importance… humour, responsibility, respect for others, interest in the world at large.'

Key facts

Charlotte's Web

First published: 1952, in the US by Harper & Brothers and in England by Hamish Hamilton Children's Books. Puffin Books reissued *Charlotte's Web* in 2014.

Illustrator: Garth Williams

Awards: The Lewis Carroll Shelf Award; Laura Ingalls Wilder Medal; the Horn Book Fanfare.

Did you know: It has sold over 45 million copies and been translated into 23 languages. It ranks 78th on the all-time bestselling hardback list.

Anticipation

Encourage the children to appreciate the anticipation of starting a new book. They should be familiar with book cover contents but revisit key features (title, author, illustrator if relevant, publisher). Explain that not all book covers or even editions contain identical information. Ask: *What other information is on the cover? Why is it there?* (For example, blurb and/or extract – to give a flavour of the contents; mini reviews – to show others have enjoyed the book; awards or sales figures – to show a book's quality or popularity; design features and illustrations – to attract readers and give clues about the genre.)

Discuss how the cover provides clues to the story without spoiling the plot. Ask: *Who are the main characters?* (Charlotte and Wilbur.) *What can you discover about them?* (Wilbur is a pig; Charlotte is a spider – they should infer this from the title and blurb.) *What genre of book do you think it is? Why?* (Animal/fantasy/adventure.) *What do you predict the story is about?* (This might depend on the edition's cover.)

There have been many covers since 1952, but some modern editions retain the original illustrator's cover. Display a variety of covers including one with visuals from the 1973/2006 films. Ask: *Which do you prefer? Why?*

Setting the scene

Read the opening paragraph. Ask: *Is this a good opening? Why?* (It's dramatic and grabs your attention – a deliberate author ploy.) Ask: *Where could he be going?* Read the rest of Chapter 1 and ask: *Which characters have been introduced?* (Fern, Mr and Mrs Arable, Avery and Wilbur.)

Read Chapters 1 to 4. Discuss why Fern wanted to save the runt. (She thought it was unfair just because he was small – an 'injustice'.) Ask: *Do you agree with Fern? Why?* The children may agree that it is cruel. Use the opportunity to talk about why animals are raised on a farm. Ask: *What sort of person is Fern? How can you tell?* (Loving,

compassionate and loyal; she saves Wilbur, looks after him, plays with him and visits him in the barn.)

Focus on how the plot is set up: Fern saves Wilbur; they become friends; Wilbur moves to the barn and misses their fun; he fails to make friends easily in his new home. Ask: *How is Wilbur feeling?* (Miserable, bored and lonely.) Stop reading just before the end of Chapter 4. Ask: *What does Wilbur want?* (A friend.) Read the final two paragraphs. Ask: *Who does the voice belong to? How do you know?* (Charlotte – the title.)

As you read, focus in on the setting. Ask: *What clues tell you where the book is set and what time of year it is?* (Springtime, the animals are with their young, the barn, Wilbur is a 'spring pig'., and so on.) Discuss springtime with the children. The cycle of life is a recurrent theme in the book.

Ask: *How does the author bring the setting and characters to life?* (Vivid descriptions: sights, smells, sounds and so on; the animals' dialogue; the animals' feelings and emotions.)

Finding a friend

Read Chapter 5 aloud. Discuss the way Wilbur speaks to Charlotte before he knows her. (Formal.) Ask: *What are Wilbur's early impressions of Charlotte?* (Beautiful and clever but he is appalled at her diet and sad she is so bloodthirsty.) Talk about making new friends and first impressions.

The problem

Refer to question 2 on the bookmark (page 12). Read Chapters 6 to 10 with the class. Ask: *What's the problem in the story that needs to be solved?* (How to save Wilbur from being slaughtered.) As the story unfolds, discuss the different farmyard characters.

Ask: *Who breaks the bad news to Wilbur and why?* (The old sheep – to cause trouble.) Compare Charlotte's reaction to Wilbur's (mature and calm versus childish and hysterical). Ask: *Are their reactions in keeping with their characters?* (Yes.)

Wilbur's problem is not the only one. Ask: *Why is Mrs Arable worried about Fern? Should she be?* (She spends too much time 'talking' to animals.)

The miracle unfolds

Talk about miracles with the class, making sure they understand the word. Invite the children to read Chapter 11. Ask: *What is the miracle?* ('SOME PIG' is written in Charlotte's web.) Ask: *Is it really a miracle in the story?* (No, the reader knows it was Charlotte's trick.) *Would it be a miracle in real life?* (If not a miracle, then still amazing.)

Based on events so far, encourage the children to predict how Charlotte will save Wilbur. (They should realise it will relate to the words in the web and their effect on humans.) Remind them that prediction is different from guessing; they must give sensible reasons to back their ideas.

Encourage the children to read on to the end of Chapter 15 and to review their predictions. Ask: *What do you think of the words chosen for Wilbur?* ('Terrific' and 'radiant'.) *Why was 'crunchy' rejected?* (It would remind the farmer of bacon.)

Re-read Chapter 15. This is a turning point in the story: on the farm (nature's inevitable cycle), for Fern and Avery (a new year at school), and for Charlotte (she is running out of time). Ask: *What did the crickets' song signify?* (The end of summer.) *How does Charlotte know she has little time left?* (Instinct.) *What does she have to do?* (Lay her egg sac and save Wilbur.)

The hour of triumph

Read Chapters 16 to 21. Note how the location changes and attention focuses on key characters: Charlotte, Wilbur and Templeton. Ask: *How does Fern change?* (She spends more time with humans than Wilbur.) *Can her mother stop worrying?* (Yes.) *Is she still Wilbur's friend?* (Yes, but now a less significant character.)

Encourage the children to predict what the 'hour of triumph' will entail. Some may predict Wilbur will win first prize. If they do, ask whether it would be fair when it is clear that Uncle is a 'superior' pig. Ask: *Why does Charlotte see it as her hour of triumph?* (She has achieved her goal.)

Point out the rollercoaster highs and lows in Chapters 19 and 20: Charlotte completing her masterpiece but admitting she won't ever see her children; Charlotte languishing – Templeton flourishing; Uncle having the blue tag – 'HUMBLE' appearing on the web; Uncle winning first prize – Wilbur being called to the judges' booth; Wilbur winning a special prize – Charlotte dying alone. Ask: *Do you think Charlotte has saved Wilbur? Why?* (Encourage reasons.) Ask: *If Wilbur had been big and strong like Uncle and won first prize, would Mr Arable still have kept him?* (Possibly not – it was the specialness Charlotte created around Wilbur that saved him.) *Did Charlotte mind dying alone?* (No – she knew Wilbur would keep her babies safe.)

The cycle renews

The climax has come and gone, the problem is resolved – so what now? Ask: *Why would the story be unfinished if it ended after Chapter 21?* (The reader does not know what happens to Charlotte's babies; Wilbur would be alone again.)

Read the final chapter aloud without stopping. Ask: *Why do you think the chapter is called 'A Warm Wind'?* (It signals the coming of spring and a new cycle of life.) *Do you think Wilbur was happy without Charlotte?* (Yes. She always held a special place in his heart but she had taught him about friendship and loyalty, and he was both friends with and loyal to her family.)

Subsequent readings

Re-read the novel to explore different aspects. Your reading does not have to be in order as children may need to refer to different parts of the story to reflect fully on some questions.

Structure

Refer to question 20 on the bookmark. Divide the book into sections to reflect the plot structure:

- Chapters 1–5: Setting the scene – Getting to know Wilbur, Fern, the farm, Templeton and Charlotte.
- Chapters 6–15: Build up – Wilbur's problem, Charlotte's problem, Fern's problem.
- Chapters 16–21: Climax and resolution – The action at the Fair – the journey signalling change: the characters return changed (except Charlotte).
- Chapter 22: Conclusion.

Point out that Chapter 15 is a pivotal chapter – it uses the crickets' song to signal summer coming to an end, symbolising the beginning of the end of things as they are. In Chapter 16, the new location and the focus on core characters is a change of tone – marking change for all of them.

Style

Refer to question 19 on the bookmark. Ask: *Who is telling the story?* (An omniscient third-person narrator who often addresses readers directly.)

As you read and re-read, encourage the children to appreciate the illustrations. The book contains a number of attractive illustrations, anthropomorphising the animals, especially Wilbur. Ask: *Do the illustrations match your idea of the characters? Why or how?* Solicit reasons to support their answers.

Setting

The story is set in America, more than 50 years ago, but any differences barely impinge on the story since the micro settings are the Arable farm, Zuckerman's barn and the County Fair.

Some children may be unfamiliar with farm life. Refer to question 9 on the bookmark. Encourage them to notice the vivid descriptions and explain any unfamiliar vocabulary or terms. Ask: *Do you know what a County Fair is?* (A gathering with competitions and events relating to farm animals and produce, accompanied by entertainment and traditional fair stalls.) *How is it similar or different to where you live?*

Characters

While there are many minor characters, the main characters dominate, especially once at the County Fair. Ask: *Who are the main characters?* (Wilbur, Charlotte and Templeton. Some may consider Fern a main character at the beginning but she fades in importance.) Ask: *What are they like?* (Charlotte: knowledgeable, wise, kind, generous and loyal; Wilbur: naïve, trusting, emotional, immature and loyal; Templeton: self-serving, greedy, and cunning.)

Refer to question 17 on the bookmark. The characters are developed in the book through their actions, appearance (illustrations and description), dialogue, comments by other characters and the narrator's comments. Show the children how these techniques are all part of building the characters bit by bit, rather than being described all at once.

Themes

Refer to questions 10 and 11 on the bookmark. Especially during the re-reading phase, help them to identify the various themes in the story and some of the symbols: friendship; loyalty; helping others; farm life; cycle of nature – life, death and time passing; the individual.

Think of proverbs, sayings or common expressions that summarise the various themes in the story: a problem shared is a problem halved; never judge a book by its cover; and so on.

SCHOLASTIC
READ & RESPOND
Bringing the best books to life in the classroom

Charlotte's Web
by E.B. White

Focus on...
Meaning

1. Why are the chapter titles significant?

2. What is the problem that needs to be solved?

3. How does Charlotte demonstrate her friendship?

4. How is nature important in the story?

5. What can we learn from the story?

Focus on...
Purpose, viewpoints and effects

6. The narrator or a character sometimes foreshadows later events. What does this mean and what effect does it have?

7. According to Charlotte, what is friendship?

8. Why is humour important in the story?

9. Was Templeton a friend to Wilbur? Why or why not?

10. What themes run through the story?

11. Which theme is the most important? Why?

SCHOLASTIC
READ & RESPOND
Bringing the best books to life in the classroom

Charlotte's Web
by E.B. White

Focus on...
Language and features

12. In what ways are words important in the story?

13. How does the author's use of our senses bring the setting to life?

14. Think of synonyms for Charlotte's words for Wilbur: 'terrific', 'radiant', 'humble'.

15. Are Charlotte's words appropriate to describe a pig?

16. Does Wilbur live up to the words?

17. What techniques does the author use to develop the characters?

18. Do the illustrations match your mental image of the characters?

Focus on...
Organisation

19. Who narrates the story? How can you tell?

20. Which chapters correspond to these story stages: introduction, build-up, climax, resolution and conclusion?

Extract 1

- Read an enlarged copy of the extract with the children following closely. Ask: *What do you notice about the five sentences following the topic sentence in paragraph one?* (They follow the same pattern: beginning with 'It…' and getting gradually longer and more descriptive.) Ask: *Which sense does the description focus on?* (Smell.) Underline the items the barn smells of.

- The pattern of the sentences changes in the second half of the paragraph. Ask: *What is unusual about how these sentences begin?* (They begin with 'And' and 'But'.) *What is the effect of this?* (It gives the impression someone is remembering more and more to add to the list.) Go through each smell and discuss whether they know that smell. If possible, let the children smell examples of different items. Notice that except for 'peaceful' (adjective), the smells are linked to nouns. Ask: *How would you describe what 'peaceful' smells like?* Get them to close their eyes and imagine feeling peaceful – what smells, sounds or feelings do they associate with it? Would it be a simile or a metaphor?

- Paragraph two focuses on visual description: what the barn feels and looks like and what's in it. Underline unfamiliar words ('scythe', 'grindstone') on your enlarged copy and encourage the children to look them up in a dictionary and discuss their use on a farm.

- The second sentence is long. Ask: *What makes the sentence long?* (The listed items in the barn.) *What indicates it is a list?* (Commas separating the nouns.) *What introduces the list?* (Colon.)

- After reading, encourage personal reflection and viewpoints. Ask: *Would you like to spend time in a barn like this? Why?*

Extract 2

- Prepare to read the extract in groups of three: narrator, Charlotte and Wilbur. Allow groups time to underline and annotate their parts to indicate where to add expression and so on. Chat to groups as they prepare. Use your enlarged version to annotate as a model, picking up points to share as you go around.

- Ask: *How do you think Wilbur is feeling?* (How would they feel?) *Is Charlotte upset by Wilbur's reaction?* (Only at the end when he calls it cruel.) Ask: *What adjectives describe Charlotte's response?* (Philosophical, rueful, resigned, feisty, irritated and offended.)

- Ask about the meaning of words in context; for example, ask what 'miserable' means and then to locate it in the text and decide if the meaning changes when combined with 'inheritance'. (Yes, although similar. It implies it is disappointing or not worth having, and so likely to cause misery.)

- Discuss why the author writes certain words in italics (to show emphasis): make the comparison with stage directions in a play.

- Tell the children reading Wilbur's part to underline the narrator's words describing how he reacts ('gasped', 'groaned', 'gloomily', 'sad'). Ask those reading Charlotte's part to underline any detail on how her voice sounds ('her pleasant, thin voice grew even thinner and more pleasant'). Looking at word level, ask: *Why are the two comparatives, 'thinner' and 'more pleasant', formed differently?* ('Pleasanter' would be three syllables, which sounds clumsy.) Ask children reading the narrator's part to underline challenging areas to read, such as the list of bugs.

- Encourage groups to exchange feedback as they practise, before finally celebrating their work with a reading performance. Experiment with a recording device for groups to review themselves performing.

SHARED READING

Extract 3

- This extract follows the story's climax and resolution. Wilbur is safe. Read an enlarged copy with the class. Ask: *What was Charlotte's main reason for saving Wilbur?* (He was her friend; she liked him.) Discuss Charlotte's secondary motive. Ask: *What does Charlotte mean by 'trying to lift up my life a trifle'?* (To make her life more noble or worthwhile.)

- Consider the use of dialogue. Ask: *How does the author recount the story here?* (Using dialogue not narrative.) *Is this more or less effective than plain narrative?* (More effective, as emotions are implied not explicit.)

- Underline informal language characteristics of the dialogue. (Contractions: 'what's', 'can't' and so on; informal expressions: 'Heaven knows', 'I'm no good', 'I'm done for'; rhetorical questions: '…what's a life, anyway?'; incomplete sentences: 'Not going back?')

- Locate the word 'trifle' in the text and in a dictionary. Discuss three possible meanings: a cold dessert of cake, fruit, custard and cream; something silly or unimportant; slightly. Ask: *What does trifle mean in this context?* (It relates to the third meaning in this context.) Ask: *What part of speech is this?* (Adverb.)

- Locate the word 'Fair'. Ask: *What part of speech is it?* (Noun.) *Why does it have a capital letter?* (Normally a common noun, but acting as a proper noun – part of the name 'County Fair'.)

- Discuss Wilbur's feelings throughout the extract. Gather adjectives ('unworthy', 'curious', 'noble', 'generous', 'nostalgic' for the farm, 'excited', 'aghast', 'horrified', 'desperate', 'anguished', 'desolate'). Identify nouns underlying any of the adjectives ('unworthiness', 'curiosity', 'nobility', 'generosity', 'nostalgia', 'excitement', 'horror', 'desperation', 'anguish', 'desolation'). Point out the different ways the adjectives turn into nouns: different word endings, addition or removal of a suffix, and so on. Distinguish the patterns in the words.

Extract 4

- Ask: *Using the heading, predict whether the extract is fact or fiction. Why?* (Factual/ information text – a 'Factfile' should contain facts.) *How does the layout suggest a factual text?* (Paragraphs with question headings. The paragraphs answer the questions.) Skim the extract to get the general idea, then read the enlarged extract paragraph by paragraph.

- **Paragraph one:** Ask: *What are the colons for in sentence 2?* (To introduce lists.) Circle the semicolon and ask its role. (To separate two parallel parts of a sentence. Point out the parallel form – two lists.) Underline the lists. (Four lists – one a list of two.) Ask: *What indicates the start of a list?* (Colon followed by parallel items, separated by commas with 'and' before the final item, or just the parallel items.) Inform that a list comprises parallel components, for example, nouns, adjectives or verbs, but not a mixture. Choose children to give examples of lists. Check for the parallel form.

- **Paragraph two:** Ask: *How sharp are spiders' eyes?* (Not very – despite the quantity.) Underline the list of senses.

- **Paragraph three:** Invite the children to list the different silks spiders use. (Dragline, sticky for trapping, wrapping up and egg sac.) Ask: *Is 'balloon' a noun or a verb in this context?* (Verb.) *How can you tell?*

- **Paragraph four:** Locate a comparison to indicate the strength of one of the spider threads. Ask: *What is the key word?* (Steel.)

- **Paragraph five:** Compare how long spiders have been around to how long Charlotte says. ('thousands and thousands of years.') Ask: *Which one is more likely to be right?* (The extract. *Charlotte's Web* is fiction: thousands of years symbolises a long time.)

- Ask the children to summarise the key information in five sentences – one per paragraph.

Extract 1

The barn was very large. It was very old. It smelled of hay and it smelled of manure. It smelled of the perspiration of tired horses and the wonderful sweet breath of patient cows. It often had a sort of peaceful smell – as though nothing bad could happen ever again in the world. It smelled of grain and of harness dressing and of axle grease and of rubber boots and of new rope. And whenever the cat was given a fish-head to eat, the barn would smell of fish. But mostly it smelled of hay, for there was always hay in the great loft up overhead. And there was always hay being pitched down to the cows and the horses and the sheep.

The barn was pleasantly warm in winter when the animals spent most of their time indoors, and it was pleasantly cool in summer when the big doors stood wide open to the breeze. The barn had stalls on the main floor for the work horses, tie-ups on the main floor for the cows, a sheepfold down below for the sheep, a pigpen down below for Wilbur, and it was full of all sorts of things that you find in barns: ladders, grindstones, pitch forks, monkey wrenches, scythes, lawn mowers, snow shovels, axe handles, milk pails, water buckets, empty grain sacks, and rusty rat traps. It was the kind of barn that swallows like to build their nests in. It was the kind of barn that children like to play in. And the whole thing was owned by Fern's uncle, Mr Homer L. Zuckerman.

Extract 2

'You mean you *eat* flies?' gasped Wilbur.

'Certainly. Flies, bugs, grasshoppers, choice beetles, moths, butterflies, tasty cockroaches, gnats, midges, daddy-long-legs, centipedes, mosquitoes, crickets – anything that is careless enough to get caught in my web. I have to live, don't I?'

'Why, yes, of course,' said Wilbur. 'Do they taste good?'

'Delicious. Of course, I don't really eat them. I drink them – drink their blood. I love blood,' said Charlotte, and her pleasant, thin voice grew even thinner and more pleasant.

'Don't say that!' groaned Wilbur. 'Please don't say things like that!'

'Why not? It's true, and I have to say what is true. I'm not entirely happy about my diet of flies and bugs, but it's the way I'm made. A spider has to pick up a living somehow or other, and I happen to be a trapper. I just naturally build a web and trap flies and other insects. My mother was a trapper before me. Her mother was a trapper before her. All our family have been trappers. Way back for thousands and thousands of years we spiders have been laying for flies and bugs.'

'It's a miserable inheritance,' said Wilbur, gloomily. He was sad because his new friend was so bloodthirsty.

'Yes, it is,' agreed Charlotte. 'But I can't help it. I don't know how the first spider in the early days of the world happened to think up this fancy idea of spinning a web, but she did, and it was clever of her, too. And since then, all of us spiders have had to work the same trick. It's not a bad pitch, on the whole.'

'It's cruel,' replied Wilbur, who did not intend to be argued out of his position.

'Well, *you* can't talk,' said Charlotte. '*You* have your meals brought to you in a pail.'

Extract 3

'Why did you do all this for me?' he asked. 'I don't deserve it. I've never done anything for you.'

'You have been my friend,' replied Charlotte. 'That in itself is a tremendous thing. I wove my webs for you because I liked you. After all, what's a life, anyway? We're born, we live a little while, we die. A spider's life can't help being something of a mess, with all this trapping and eating flies. By helping you, perhaps I was trying to lift up my life a trifle. Heaven knows anyone's life can stand a little of that.'

'Well,' said Wilbur, 'I'm no good at making speeches. I haven't got your gift for words. But you have saved me, Charlotte, and I would gladly give my life for you – I really would.'

'I'm sure you would. And I thank you for your generous sentiments.'

'Charlotte,' said Wilbur. 'We're all going home today. The Fair is almost over. Won't it be wonderful to be back home in the barn cellar again with the sheep and the geese? Aren't you anxious to get home?'

For a moment Charlotte said nothing. Then she spoke in a voice so low Wilbur could hardly hear the words.

'I will not be going back to the barn,' she said.

Wilbur leapt to his feet. 'Not going back?' he cried. 'Charlotte, what are you talking about?'

'I'm done for,' she replied. 'In a day or two I'll be dead. I haven't even strength enough to climb down into the crate. I doubt if I have enough silk in my spinneret to lower me to the ground.'

Hearing this, Wilbur threw himself down in an agony of pain and sorrow. Great sobs racked his body. He heaved and grunted with desolation. 'Charlotte,' he moaned. 'Charlotte! My true friend!'

Extract 4

Spiders factfile

1. WHAT ARE SPIDERS?

Spiders and insects are both invertebrates, with a body protected by a hard exoskeleton. Insects have six legs and three body parts: head, abdomen and thorax; whereas spiders are arachnids with 8 legs and 2 body parts: cephalothorax and abdomen. The cephalothorax is the head and thorax as one, containing the eyes, mouthparts and four pairs of legs. Scorpions, ticks and mites are also arachnids.

2. HOW DO SPIDERS SEE?

Most spiders have eight simple eyes. Although eight eyes may seem advantageous, most spiders cannot see well and rely on other senses to find their prey, such as touch, vibration and taste.

3. WHAT IS SPIDER SILK?

Spider silk is a protein squeezed out of spinnerets as a liquid, which then hardens. Spiders use a variety of silks for different purposes. The dragline and sticky thread is used for webs, but a different silk is used to wrap up prey and another to make the egg sac. To spread out from their birth place, infant spiders often float or balloon on the wind using long, silk threads.

4. HOW DO SPIDERS SPIN WEBS?

First, the spider creates a framework of strong thread (dragline) radiating out from the centre and attached to plants, trees, doorways or anything strong enough to support the web. Once the frame is ready, the spider works back towards the centre, spinning a spiral of sticky threads to catch its prey. The sticky threads are elastic but the dragline thread is stronger – stronger than a thread of steel of the same width.

5. WHERE ARE SPIDERS FOUND?

Having been around for more than 2 million years, spiders are found all over the world in all sorts of habitats, from the coast to the jungle: on the ground, under rocks, on plants, in trees and so on. Antarctica is the only continent without spiders. Can you suggest why?stronger than a thread of steel of the same width.

1. Making links

To link ideas across sentences and paragraphs using adverbials.

What you need

Copies of *Charlotte's Web*.

What to do

- Check the children's recall of the purpose of adverbials to link sentences, especially of time and order. Practise with a brief set of instructions, for example: First, open Charlotte's Web. Second, turn to the beginning of Chapter 5. Third, locate the illustration of Charlotte. Ask: *What other adverbials could be used instead of 'second' and 'third'?* ('Next', 'then', 'finally', 'lastly'.)

- Together, read the text describing how Charlotte catches a fly, starting ''First,' said Charlotte…' Ask: *Which adverbials does she use?* ('First', 'next', 'now'.) *Where are the adverbials? What do they link*? (At or close to the front of a paragraph. They link paragraphs.) Demonstrate how each stage is a paragraph, so paragraphs rather than sentences are sequenced.

- In Chapter 13, read the two paragraphs, from 'Charlotte climbed to a point…' to 'very busy helping.'

- Invite the children to summarise Charlotte's actions writing 'TERRIFIC' in her web into two short paragraphs, using adverbials of time and place to link ideas both within and across the paragraphs. Demonstrate that summarising requires only important words and actions, not all the detail.

Differentiation

Support: Provide a frame of adverbials to help children summarise:
Paragraph 1: First… Next… Then… Finally…
Paragraph 2: After that… Then… Lastly…
Extension: Ask children to summarise a longer part to include writing 'R' in the web up to 'Then she slept'. Suggest they summarise the numerous short steps into two or three sentences using adverbials in a third paragraph.

2. able or ible?

Objective

To master words ending in 'able' and 'ible' or 'ably' and 'ibly'.

What you need

Photocopiable page 22 'Sort your 'ibles' from your 'ables'', interactive activity ''ible' or 'able'?'.

What to do

- Both the 'ible' and 'able' suffixes mean 'able to be'. For example, 'visible' means able to be seen.

- Charlotte thinks humans are 'gullible'. Write the word on the board spelled 'gullible' and 'gullable'. Ask which is correct.

- Hold a quick spelling bee, with children guessing whether these words end in 'ible' or 'able': 'responsible', 'knowledgeable', 'legible', 'reliable', 'dependable', 'horrible'. Ask: *How did you choose?* (Sound, prior knowledge, guess.) *What word class are these words?* (Adjectives.)

- Using photocopiable page 22 'Sort your 'ibles' from your 'ables'', ask the children to underline the suffixes. Ask: *What do you notice about the root word or stem in questions 1–4?* (They are complete or recognisable words.) *What spelling rules are used when adding the suffix?* (No change to root, drop final 'e', change 'y' to 'i', double final consonant (usually only 't', 'g', 'b', 'm', 'p').)

- Ask: *What do you notice about the root or stem in the 'ible' list?* (Not complete words. Note that there are exceptions: 'accessible', 'digestible', 'flexible'.)

- Challenge the class to predict the spelling rule to change 'able' and 'ible' adjectives into adverbs. (Drop the final 'e' and add 'ly': terrible/terribly; understandable/understandably.)

Differentiation

Support: Give children additional practice, using interactive activity ''ible' or 'able'?'.
Extension: Challenge children to search for additional words that follow each rule and experiment with inventing new 'able' words, such as 'emailable', 'giffable' and 'jpeggable'.

3. Challenging punctuation

Objective

To use the semicolon, colon and dash to mark the boundary between independent clauses.

What you need

Copies of *Charlotte's Web*, photocopiable page 23 'Extend your punctuation', interactive activity 'Make a mark'.

What to do

- Check the children are familiar with the appearance and names of the colon, semicolon and dash (not to be confused with a hyphen). They may be familiar with colons introducing a list and marking off speakers in dialogue or playscripts, semicolons in lists, and dashes as parentheses. Introduce further roles for each mark.

  - **Colons** introduce lists, speakers and so on. They can also introduce a second clause into a sentence that adds information or understanding to the first one. For example: We love Charlotte: she's our hero.
  - **Semicolons** can work with or as conjunctions between two closely related clauses of equal weight. The semicolon precedes a conjunction adverb or replaces it. For example: Spiders eat bugs; however, pigs eat slops. Spiders eat bugs; pigs eat slops. The effect is slightly different.
  - **Dashes** separate additional information that is related but inessential, such as an afterthought or an aside. For example: Charlotte is a grey spider – some might say a beautiful one.

- Ask children to work in pairs on photocopiable page 23. They should decide whether to add a colon, semicolon or dash to join the pairs of sentences or clauses. Remind them to cross out words, if necessary, such as conjunctions.

Differentiation

Support: Give children additional practise by using the interactive activity 'Make a mark'.
Extension: Invite children to scan *Charlotte's Web* for examples of colons, semicolons and dashes. Challenge them to invent their own sentences following similar patterns.

4. Possible or impossible?

Objective

To indicate degrees of possibility using adverbs and modal verbs.

What you need

Printable page 'Endless possibilities', scissors.

What to do

- Draw an arrow on the board with 'likely' just before the tip and 'unlikely' at the other end. Ask a variety of questions and invite the class to predict where the answers lie on the scale. Encourage them to use these words to modify 'likely': 'hardly', 'slightly', 'quite', 'fairly', 'surely', 'very', 'definitely'. Ask: *What part of speech are they?* (Adverbs.) Possible questions include:
  - Will Templeton do something kind for Wilbur?
  - Will Charlotte save Wilbur?
  - Will the 'dud' goose egg break?
  - Do animals talk?

- Discuss modal verbs together. Explain that they are auxiliary verbs that express possibility ('could', 'can', 'will', 'must', 'might', 'may', 'shall'), necessity ('need to', 'must'), obligation ('should' – implies it might not happen, 'must') or ability ('can', 'cannot'). The children will already use them but may not have understood how they work. Modal verbs are always followed by another infinitive and they do not add an 's' for third person.

- Working in groups, challenge the children to invent statement clusters indicating degrees of possibility. Start with an example: Wilbur could win a prize. Wilbur might win a prize. Wilbur will win a prize.

Differentiation

Support: Tell the children to cut out the cards from the printable page and sequence them in different groups ('perhaps', 'probably', 'certainly'). They can use these to help invent sentences expressing possibility.
Extension: Ask pairs to invent a dialogue using as many adverbs and modal verbs as they can. Encourage them to experiment with verbs indicating necessity, obligation and ability.

5. Bullet it!

Objective

To punctuate bullet points correctly.

What you need

Extract 1, copies of *Charlotte's Web*.

What to do

- Revise how to create a list in a sentence. Ask: *How do you separate items in a simple list?* (Using commas, with 'and' separating the last two items.) Consolidate with an example: 'Charlotte was wise, kind, loyal and a true friend.'

- Discuss using semicolons to separate more complex list items, to avoid ambiguity. For example: Wilbur loved: slops; oatmeal; doughnuts; and bread and butter pudding.

- Check the children know what bullet points are. Turn to Extract 1 and locate the list starting 'The barn had stalls…'. Ask: *How can you tell it's a list?* (Commas between successive nouns.)

- Ask: *How do you write a shopping list?* (Down not across.) Ask: *Why would you use bullets?* (To see each list item clearly.)

- Put some example lists on the board and ask children for additional items to grasp parallel form.

  Charlotte told Wilbur to:
  - pull himself together
  - stop crying
  - settle down.

  Spring was symbolised by the following:
  - Goslings hatching.
  - Crops growing in the fields.
  - Lambs being born.

- Ask: *Why is the punctuation different in the two lists?* (No capitals or end punctuation in the first list (until the end) because each item flows from the stem sentence ending in 'to:'. No stem sentence in the second list.)

- Ask children to rewrite the sentence in Chapter 11 beginning 'The Zuckermans' driveway…' to include a bulleted list. Remind them to include the colon and to remove 'and' words.

6. Salutations!

Objective

To note the differences in formal and informal speech and writing.

What you need

Copies of *Charlotte's Web*, photocopiable page 24 'Formal or informal?', interactive activity 'More or less formal'.

What to do

- Exchange a formal greeting, say 'Good morning' or 'Good afternoon', with the class. Ask: *Is this how you greet your friends?* (Unlikely.) *How do you greet them?* (Expect a wide range of responses.)

- As a class, discuss different greetings and ways of speaking and in what context they occur. Ask: *Do you speak to your teacher in the same way as your friends? How is it different?* (No. Likely to include casual words, slang, idiomatic expressions versus more careful, formal words and sentence construction.) Emphasise that informal language does not imply disrespectful language.

- Read Chapter 5 together from where Wilbur tries to find his new friend ('Attention, please!' to 'But just call me Charlotte.'). Ask: *Why does Wilbur speak so formally?* (He wants to make a good impression.) Ask: *Is Charlotte's greeting formal or informal?* (Salutations – formal.)

- Open interactive activity 'More or less formal' and work through it together as a warm-up. Then hand out photocopiable page 24 'Formal or informal?' for the children to practise rewriting sentences using different levels of formality. Remind them that dialogue is usually less formal than narrative because it reflects actual conversations.

Differentiation

Support: Let the children work through the photocopiable sheet orally in groups, or just complete the first two exercises.

Extension: Invite the children to use a thesaurus to find synonyms of the same level of formality to use in their rewrites.

Sort your 'ibles' from your 'ables'

- Underline the suffix in each word and write the root word next to it.
- Write the spelling rule used to form the words.

1. reasonable _____

   Rule: _____

2. reliable _____

   Rule: _____

3. forgettable _____

   Rule: _____

4. believable _____

   Rule: _____

- Add the suffix 'ible' to each word stem below to form a word.

5. terr_____   7. vis_____

6. incred_____   8. imposs_____

- Write down a difference between the 'ible' and 'able' words that could help you remember which suffix to choose.

_____

- Fill in the blanks below using a suitable 'ible' or 'able' word.

Wilbur thought that Charlotte was very wise and _____.

He knew she would be _____ of saving him from his

_____ fate. Meanwhile, Charlotte decided 'crunchy' was not

a _____ word to write in her web because it made Wilbur

sound so deliciously _____.

Extend your punctuation

Colons introduce lists or a clause that adds information or understanding to the first one.

Semicolons can work <u>with</u> or <u>as</u> conjunctions to link two closely related clauses of equal weight.

Dashes separate off additional information or a comment.

● Choose whether to add a colon, semicolon or dash in each space below.

1. Charlotte's purpose was clear_____ no one would eat Wilbur.

2. I enjoyed *Charlotte's Web*_____ although it was partly sad.

3. Wilbur thought about his favourite foods_____ meat scraps, apples, acorns and milky bread.

4. I may as well go to the Fair_____ some say it's a Rat's Paradise.

5. Charlotte is thoughtful and kind_____ Templeton is not.

● Write five sentences of your own following the pattern of the sentences above.

_____

_____

_____

_____

_____

● Add a colon, semicolon or dash to make sense of these sentences.

6. The competition was over Uncle had won first prize.

7. Charlotte left Wilbur a final gift she left him her children.

8. I love life in the barn I even like Templeton sometimes.

Formal or informal?

- Synonyms are words that have a similar meaning. Match the formal and informal synonyms and then circle the informal synonym.

discard	formal	occupation	failed	posh
throw	tell	inform		beverage
hi	enquire	ask	job	flunked
		hello	drink	

- Rewrite these informal expressions in more formal language.

1. Shut up! _____

2. Keep your hair on. _____

3. What's up? _____

4. Need a hand? _____

- Rewrite the underlined words using formal language.

5. 'Charlotte, <u>you're on fire</u>, with all your words for Wilbur!'

   _____

6. 'Templeton, will you come to the Fair?' '<u>Not a chance</u>!'

   _____

- Suggest ways to write these expressions more informally.

7. Thank you very much. You are most kind.

   _____

8. Please accept my sincere apologies.

   _____

9. I am unable to believe what you say.

   _____

1. Cast the characters

Objective

To draw up character profiles.

What you need

Copies of *Charlotte's Web*, printable page 'Casting cards', scissors.

What to do

- Challenge to see who can list, one on each line, the most characters in the novel from memory. Let them check each other's lists and add missing ones.

- Next to each character, ask the children to write a couple of descriptive adjectives, with each adjective backed by evidence from the book. Give them an example, such as: The oldest sheep: mean – she told Wilbur what was in store for him. Ask for children to volunteer their adjectives and evidence.

- Now get them to categorise the characters' importance to the plot using stars: *** for major (Wilbur, Charlotte, Templeton and Fern); ** for minor (the goose, the oldest sheep, Homer Zuckerman and Mrs Arable); * for background (Lurvy, Mr Arable, Dr Dorian and so on).

- Ask: *How did you measure each character's importance?* Encourage questions such as: *Could the storyline happen without the character? Do they add humour? Do they do or say something important? Do they engage your feelings?* (Like, dislike, empathy and so on.)

- Hand out printable page 'Casting cards' to groups of four and ask them to imagine they are casting for a play of *Charlotte's Web*. They must draw up character profiles so people auditioning know how to act. Each group member should cut out and complete profile cards for at least one major and one minor character.

Differentiation

Support: Ask children to just complete one character profile – major or minor.

Extension: Hold auditions. The children can give each other the casting cards and rate each other's performances on how well they interpreted the profile card.

2. Templeton – villain or hero?

Objective

To infer characters' feelings, thoughts and motives.

What you need

Copies of *Charlotte's Web*, notebooks.

What to do

- In Chapter 4, read the section where Wilbur asks Templeton to play. Ask: *What would Templeton prefer to do?* (Eating, gnawing, spying, hiding.)

- Ask for volunteers to describe Templeton's character using evidence from the story. (Words used to describe him: 'sourly', 'stealthily', 'crafty', 'skill' and 'cunning', 'sharp nose'. His favourite activities. The way he speaks. His secret tunnels.)

- Tell the children to scan Chapter 6 and note down anything further they discover about Templeton's character. Encourage them to notice how the author builds his character: his wanting the dud egg; the gander's warning; the narrator telling the reader what the animals know. Ask: *Is Templeton a villain in the story?* Ask for evidence from the book.

- Together, list how Templeton helps. Then ask: *What is his motive each time?* (Gets string – for a laugh; stores dud egg [which saves Charlotte when it breaks] – for his own collection; finds new words – to protect his food supply; goes to the Fair – to find the 'rat's paradise'; revives Wilbur at the Fair – to ensure his food supply back at the farm; collects the egg sac – unclear motivation, possibly his redeeming moment?)

- Ask: *How do characters take advantage of Templeton's nature?* (They know he'll do what they want if there's something in it for him.) *Is this fair?* (Answers will vary – elicit reasons.) In reality, Templeton is a kind of antihero – he was vital in helping to save Wilbur, but he didn't do it to help.

- Invite the children to write a paragraph about Templeton, giving their opinion on whether he is a hero or a villain in the story.

3. Charlotte A Cavatica

Objective

To write for real purposes (a tribute).

What you need

Copies of *Charlotte's Web*, photocopiable page 29 'A tribute', media resources 'Spider diagram' and 'Small ads'.

Cross-curricular link

PSHE

What to do

- Start the class by reading Wilbur's thoughts after meeting Charlotte at the end of Chapter 5. Invite the children to remember meeting one of their friends for the first time. What were their first impressions? Ask: *Do you need to know someone a long time to know them well?* (No, but you do need shared experiences.)

- Ask: *How long did Wilbur know Charlotte?* (Spring and summer.) *What did he find out about her in that short time?* List their responses on the board, or use media resource 'Spider diagram', using two different colours to separate Charlotte's capabilities from her character traits. For example: capabilities include spinning webs, trapping flies; character traits include being bloodthirsty, thoughtful, generous.

- Hand out photocopiable page 29. Ask: *What is a tribute?* (Something that you do or say to show that you respect and admire someone, especially in a formal situation or if someone has died.) Invite the children to fill in the sheet, imagining they are Wilbur writing a tribute to Charlotte after she has died. Remind them to include Wilbur's thoughts and reflections, not their own.

Differentiation

Support: Encourage the children to use the class list from the board to help them.

Extension: Invite the children to create a 'Wanted' classified advertisement for the perfect friend (for Wilbur). Use media resource 'Small ads' to give children an idea of style and layout.

4. Map the plot

Objective

To identify and discuss conventions in and across writing.

What you need

Copies of *Charlotte's Web*, paper bookmarks, photocopiable page 30 'Map the plot', interactive activity 'Sequence the plot'.

What to do

- Briefly remind children of the classic story structure and write the stages on the board: introduction, problem, build-up, climax, resolution and conclusion.

- Discuss the plot of *Charlotte's Web* together. Ask a range of questions (see below), referencing each part in the book. Get the children to jot down notes on paper bookmarks and slip them into their own copies to mark the plot progression, such as the introduction of a character, or setting the scene.

- Direct your questions to show how closely the author follows the classic story structure. Ask: *What happens in the first few chapters? When do we meet the main characters?* (Charlotte appears at the end of Chapter 4.) *What is the setting? When does it change?* (Arable farm, the barn, the Fair, back to the barn.) Point out how the setting change signals a new phase in the story. Ask: *What is the problem? How is it introduced? What leads up to and signals the climax? How is the problem resolved? What loose ends must be tied up?*

- Hand out photocopiable page 30 'Map the plot' and ask the children to complete the sheet independently, using their bookmarks to locate the different elements of the story.

Differentiation

Support: Encourage children to match parts of the story to the plot structure using the interactive activity 'Sequence the plot'.

Extension: Ask the children to translate their plot map into paragraphs, summarising the key elements of the plot. Encourage adverbials and other cohesion devices to link paragraphs.

5. Opposites attract

Objective

To summarise the main ideas.

What you need

Copies of *Charlotte's Web*, thesaurus, printable page 'Character web'.

What to do

- Start the class by asking: *Who is older, Charlotte or Wilbur?* They are likely to assume Charlotte is older than Wilbur but in reality they were probably much the same age. Ask: *Why does Charlotte seem so much older than Wilbur?* (She matured quickly because she has a short life span.)

- Hand out the printable page 'Character web' and organise the children into pairs to create character maps – one for Charlotte and one for Wilbur (add name to centre of the web). Then ask them to write adjectives to describe Charlotte/Wilbur in the first row. In the second row they should add more interesting synonyms (using a thesaurus). Start them off with an example: *mature*; *naïve*.

- In the third row, ask children to add examples of things the characters do, say or think, to support their chosen adjectives. For example: *intelligent – Charlotte knows difficult words, such as 'gullible'*. Encourage them to discuss each other's character webs and make suggestions for things to add.

- Explain that they must now use their maps to draw up a simple 'similarities and differences' table to compare the characters.

- Complete the session by asking whether Charlotte and Wilbur change during the story and if so how. (Wilbur changes more than Charlotte as he learns about friendship.)

Differentiation

Support: Let the children complete just the adjective and synonyms parts of the character web.

Extension: Ask the children to write a short paragraph explaining why they think Charlotte and Wilbur became friends, despite their differences.

6. Face facts

Objective

To distinguish between statements of fact and opinion.

What you need

Interactive activity 'Fact or opinion', Extract 4, photocopiable page 31 'Fact or opinion', scissors.

Cross-curricular links

History, science

What to do

- Ask the children to explain the difference between a fact and an opinion. Explain that a fact is something known to be true or can be shown to have happened or existed. An opinion is a personal view or judgement, often based on feelings as much as facts.

- Ask them to write definitions in their own words. Share everyone's definitions and build a class definition before checking in a dictionary. Discuss contexts that require facts rather than opinions, for example history research or science experiments.

- Work through interactive activity 'Fact or opinion' as a class. Then put up an enlarged version of Extract 4. Ask: *Does this text contain mostly statements of fact or opinion?* (Fact.)

- Ask pairs to write two statements each about Charlotte – one factual statement and one opinion. Ask them to swap their statements and see whether they agree.

- Hand out photocopiable page 31 'Fact or opinion'. Tell the children to cut out the cards and categorise them as statements of fact or opinion. When finished, invite them to complete the blank cards with their own fact and opinion statements to then give to a partner to categorise correctly.

Differentiation

Support: Let the children just sort the given statements rather than writing their own.

Extension: Ask the children to research a species of spider and either write a factfile or a paragraph explaining whether they like spiders.

7. Location, location, location

Objective

To summarise the main ideas drawn from more than one paragraph.

What you need

Copies of *Charlotte's Web*, media resources 'On the farm' and 'Plan of barn', poster paper, colouring pens or paints, collage materials (optional).

Cross-curricular link

Art and design

What to do

- Read Chapter 3 up until Mrs Zuckerman notices Wilbur has escaped. Ask: *What is the purpose of this part of the chapter?* (To introduce the main setting of the book.) *How is it different to the way the characters are introduced?* (Descriptive narrative rather than dialogue, thoughts and actions.)

- Show the images on media resource 'On the farm' of a farmyard, barn, apple orchard and vegetable garden. Ask: *How does the setting in the book seem similar or different?* List their observations on the board.

- Explain that they are going to sketch the story's setting on poster paper, based on the author's description in the chapter. Re-read the chapter and, while reading, tell the children to close their eyes to visualise the setting: the barn and its different sections, Wilbur's yard outside, the sheepfold, the grass, the vegetable garden and the apple orchard.

- Get the class into small groups and hand out rough paper for them to sketch their ideas first before collecting their poster paper for their final version.

Differentiation

Support: Encourage the children to skim through the book's illustrations depicting the setting for ideas. Let them use the media resource 'Plan of barn' to guide them.

Extension: Encourage the children to bring the farmyard to life with colours, paints or collage materials.

8. Who solved the problem?

Objective

To ask questions to improve their understanding.

What you need

Copies of *Charlotte's Web*, printable pages 'Who, what, why, when, where, how?' and 'Cool questions'.

What to do

- Open by asking: *Who solved Wilbur's problem*? If they say Charlotte, ask them who helped her and how. (Templeton, the farmyard animals, Wilbur.)

- Revise the key question words: 'who', 'what', 'when', 'where', 'why' and 'how'. Explain their usefulness in extending thinking and in checking understanding. For example, they might know **who** solved Wilbur's problem but do they know **why** each character helped or **how, where** and **when**?

- Demonstrate that some questions have right/ wrong or yes/no answers and these are called 'closed' questions. However, others require thinking, judgement or opinion and these are called 'open' questions. For example: *Did Charlotte solve Wilbur's problem?* (Closed.) What *was her motive?* (Open.)

- Hand out printable page 'Who, what, why, when, where, how?' for the children to complete.

- Invite them to choose a favourite episode in the story and come up with five questions to deepen their understanding of how the episode is important to the plot. Encourage them to notice whether their questions are 'open' or 'closed'.

- Tell the children to find a partner, swap sheets and answer each other's questions, using full sentences, backed by reasons where necessary.

Differentiation

Support: They can use printable page 'Cool questions' as an outline.

Extension: Encourage the children to develop broader open questions, focusing on themes. Ask: *Why is friendship so important in the story?* Let them exchange questions and answers.

A tribute

● Fill in Wilbur's tribute to Charlotte after she has died. Use full sentences as much as possible and write in a formal but personal style.

Charlotte A Cavatica

A friendship quote:

_____

How we met:

_____

How we became friends:

_____

Things we shared or did together (memories, favourite things):

_____

_____

_____

Charlotte's talents:

_____

Adjectives that describe her best qualities:

_____

Charlotte's accomplishments (what she achieved):

_____

What I will miss about her:

_____

_____

_____

The last time I saw her:

_____

Thank you Charlotte for…

_____

_____

Map the plot

● Use your bookmarks to map events in the plot.

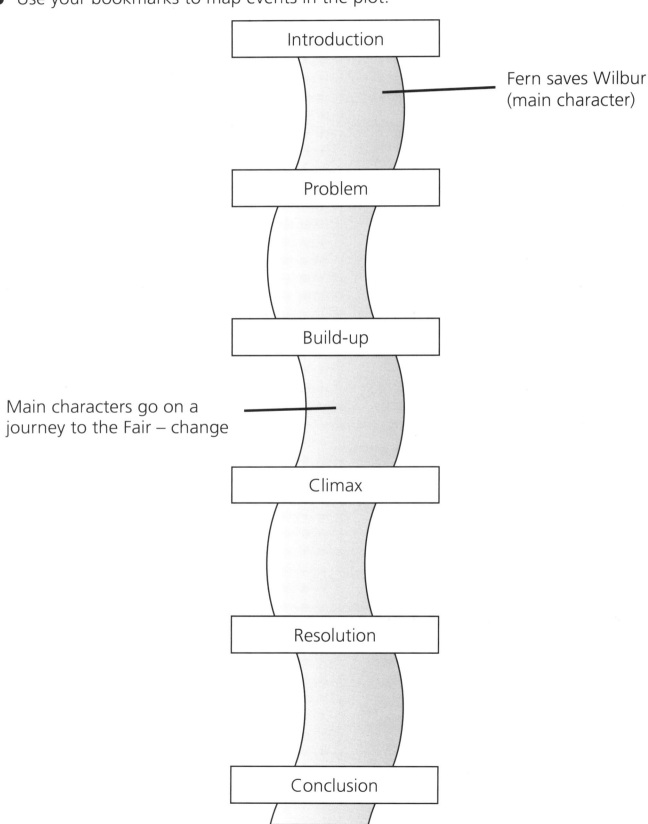

Introduction

Fern saves Wilbur (main character)

Problem

Build-up

Main characters go on a journey to the Fair – change

Climax

Resolution

Conclusion

Fact or opinion

● Cut out these cards. Sort each statement into either fact or opinion.

Charlotte is a barn spider.	Charlotte is very talented.
Wilbur's crate was magnificent.	Lurvy looked after Wilbur at the Fair.
Uncle was a superior pig to Wilbur.	Templeton is a hero not a villain.
Wilbur was packed in a crate with gold letters.	Henry Fussy went on the big wheel with Fern.
The old sheep told Wilbur something troubling.	Flies' blood is delicious.
Pigs make excellent pets.	Black pigs are the cutest.
Wilbur is humble.	Farmers like eating ham.
Mrs Arable consulted Dr Dorian about Fern.	Most people hate spiders.

TALK ABOUT IT

1. I am me

Objective

To talk about individuality (different skills).

What you need

Copies of *Charlotte's Web*, old magazines and newspaper inserts.

Cross-curricular link

Citizenship

What to do

- Read the first part of Chapter 9 'Wilbur's Boast'. Ask: *Why did Wilbur want to spin a web?* (He wanted to be like Charlotte.) *Why couldn't he spin one?* (He had neither spinnerets nor know-how.) *Did it make him less valuable than Charlotte?* (No.) *Did Wilbur need to spin a web?* (No.) *Why not?* (He didn't have to trap his own food.)

- Ask for volunteers to give an example of something they can do but others can't and vice versa. Have a class discussion on why we need people with different talents. Remind the class to listen attentively to people's ideas and to follow up each other's thoughts by contributing ideas along the same lines or in contrast, rather than just saying what they want to say without reference to the discussion.

- In pairs, ask the children to think of something special or unique they are good at – a talent. If they cannot think of something, invite the partner to suggest any talents based on their knowledge.

- Hand out magazines for pairs to skim through to choose two or three words they would 'spin into a web' to describe each other. Ask them to cut them out to give to their partners, accompanied by an oral explanation of why they chose them.

Differentiation

Support: Ask the children to choose just one word for each other.

Extension: Tell the children to prepare a short speech to present to the class explaining the words they have chosen for their partners. Their speeches must include reasons and examples.

2. Role play an interview

Objective

To interview a character to find out how they feel.

What you need

Photocopiable page 35 'My interview', copies of *Charlotte's Web*.

What to do

- Start by asking the class who they would most like to meet, for example, sports personalities, politicians or celebrities. Allow five minutes for them to think of three questions they would ask them in an interview. Share their questions.

- Ask: *Which character would you most like to meet in* Charlotte's Web*? Why?* (Make sure they give reasons for their choice.)

- Explain that they are going to interview Wilbur or Charlotte (they can choose) at the end of the story, for the local television station. They should perform their interviews as a role play, one child playing the interviewer and the other playing the character.

- Hand out photocopiable page 35 and ask pairs to complete the questions and answers to help them remember what to say in the role play later on. To get ideas going, share the answers to a couple of starter questions, such as: *Wilbur, how did it feel when you won the prize? Charlotte, how did you feel when Wilbur won his prize?* Remind them to get in character and imagine what the characters would have been thinking. For example: *How did Charlotte feel about being left alone? What was Wilbur thinking on the way home?*

- Once they have finished their questions and answers, ask them to practise their role plays before presenting them.

Differentiation

Support: Help pairs invent suitable questions for them to answer.

Extension: Encourage pairs to learn their role play well enough to perform it without notes. Encourage ad-libbing, as well as expressions and manner of speaking suitable to the characters.

3. How was the Fair?

Objective

To explain and discuss understanding of what they have read from different characters' perspectives.

What you need

Dictionaries, media resource 'Different perspectives', copies of *Charlotte's Web*.

Cross-curricular links

Art and design, citizenship

What to do

- Introduce the word 'perspective'. Ask the children to look it up in their dictionaries and discuss its different meanings (the way you think about something; a way of drawing things to appear realistic in size and position).

- Open the media resource 'Different perspectives'. Display the first set of images (road leading away) and ask: *How does this picture show perspective?* (Path lines come closer and bushes get smaller towards the horizon.) Display the second image (looking up) and ask: *From what perspective was this taken?* (Ground up, top down and so on.) Display the third image (two views of the same scene) and ask: *What do you notice about these images?* (Same view from different perspectives.)

- Organise the children into groups (mixed ability if possible) and invite each group member to choose a character: Fern, Charlotte, Templeton, Wilbur, Mr Zuckerman or Lurvy.

- Explain that they are going to tell each other about their experiences at the Fair from the perspective of their chosen character. Allow some time for the children to skim through the Fair chapters focusing on their character: what they did, how they felt, whether they enjoyed it and so on. They can jot down notes to help them remember.

- Ask the groups to begin telling each other about their Fair experience. If necessary, demonstrate in character yourself or ask a confident child.

4. A friend in need

Objective

To link back to their own experience.

What you need

Extract 3, photocopiable page 36 'Self-reflection', recording device (optional).

Cross-curricular link

Citizenship

What to do

- Re-read Extract 3 on Charlotte's reasons for helping Wilbur. Ask: *How did Charlotte benefit from helping Wilbur?* (It lifted her life a trifle.) Encourage the class to explain in their own words what Charlotte meant. Compare this to Templeton helping Wilbur. Why did he do it? How did he benefit? Ask: *Do you need good motives to help someone?* (No. Templeton helped to save Wilbur whatever his motives.)

- Encourage the class to think of other books where one character helps another. Ask: *Who helped whom? How? What was their motive?* It's important to encourage children to look beyond actions to motives, as it helps them infer character information and read beyond the literal.

- Having established examples of characters helping each other, ask: *How did helping make these characters feel?* It is unlikely to be explicit in the text but discuss implicit signs, such as feelings, character growth, things they say or do, what the narrator says and so on.

- Invite the children to remember an occasion when they helped someone. Hand out photocopiable page 36 'Self-reflection' for them to complete. Give them a personal example as a model.

- They must now use their reflections to prepare a one- to two-minute presentation on their personal experience of helping someone. Consider recording the presentations to improve their delivery.

5. Save our spiders!

Objective

To give a persuasive talk.

What you need

Extract 4, interactive activity 'Phobias', printable pages 'Barn spider factfile' and 'Be persuasive', copies of *Charlotte's Web*.

Cross-curricular links

Science, geography

What to do

- Write 'arachnophobia' on the board. Ask: *What does it mean?* (Fear of spiders.) Tell the class to scan for a word in Extract 4 ('arachnid') to help work it out and hold a straw poll to see how many of the class are arachnophobes.

- Ask: *Do you know any other phobia (fear) words?* Mention a few unusual phobias and then open interactive activity 'Phobias', asking children to match phobias to their meanings.

- Display the printable page 'Barn spider factfile'. Re-read Chapter 9 where Charlotte describes her leg. Ask: *How accurately is Charlotte portrayed in the book?* (Very accurately: looks, habitat, prey, lifespan, value in ecosystem.) Ask: *Does* Charlotte's Web *teach us about spiders and their value in the environment?* (Yes – if accurate, stories can also teach.)

- Give pairs 15 minutes to come up with a persuasive talk to give to a younger class on the importance of protecting spiders, printable page 'Barn and spider factfile' and *Charlotte's Web*.

- Hand out printable page 'Be persuasive' as a reminder of useful techniques.

Differentiation

Support: Suggest one or two techniques and facts for children to use.

Extension: Allow the children to do further research on the value of spiders and to orally feedback their findings to the class, who can make notes.

6. Tell me a story

Objective

To tell or recount a story.

What you need

Copies of *Charlotte's Web*, magazines with pictures, photocopiable page 37 'Storyboard (1)'.

What to do

- Read the end of Chapter 13 where Wilbur asks Charlotte to tell him a story. Ask: *Is her story true or fiction?* (The author presents it as a true story but of course it is fiction.) *Do you think the events really happened exactly as Charlotte said? Why*? (Probably not.) Stories often have exaggerated events and elaborated detail for interest – truth is less important in a storytelling context.

- Ask: *Does Charlotte's story follow the standard story pattern? How?* Encourage thoughtful responses linking events in the story to stages in the structure.

- Ask: *How would a journalist have told the story differently?* (More accurate and factual, with less dramatic detail.) Ask the children to invent headlines to match the story. Remind them about techniques such as alliteration and double meanings for words. Have fun with this activity.

- Hand out magazines and ask the children to choose a picture to give to a partner (it doesn't have to be of people, it could be animals or scenery for a setting). Then tell them to invent a story around each other's pictures using photocopiable page 37 'Storyboard (1)' to remind them about story structure and features, such as dialogue, vivid description and so on.

Differentiation

Support: Let the children make up a story together based on a chosen picture.

Extension: Encourage the children to suggest improvements to each other's stories and to practise a revised version to tell to other pairs or the class.

My interview

Interviewee: _____ Interviewer: _____

Question: _____

Answer: _____

_____

_____

Question: _____

Answer: _____

_____

_____

Question: _____

Answer: _____

_____

_____

Question: _____

Answer: _____

_____

_____

Question: _____

Answer: _____

_____

_____

Notes:

Self-reflection

Person I helped

Why I helped

How I helped

How the person reacted

How it made me feel

How I think the person felt after being helped

Why I think it is important to be a 'friend in need' society

Storyboard (1)

● Use the frames to plan a story around a picture. Describe or draw key events and below each frame, add dialogue ideas.

1. Introduce characters	2. Set the scene
Dialogue	Dialogue

3. Introduce problem	4. Build-up
Dialogue	Dialogue

5. Climax	6. Resolution
Dialogue	Dialogue

GET WRITING

1. How to kill a fly

Objective

To read and write for real purposes.

What you need

Copies of *Charlotte's Web*, interactive activity 'Sequencing instructions', poster paper.

Cross-curricular link

Science

What to do

- Start by asking the children to give oral instructions to each other on how to do something simple, such as starting up the computer, making a sandwich or tidying their room. Build a checklist of the features of instructions on a piece of poster paper to go on the classroom wall: title stating aim, what you need, sequenced steps (using numbers or time connectives), imperative (bossy) verbs, easy-to-understand language, only necessary detail.

- Ask: *Where do we encounter instructions in everyday life?* (Recipes, science experiments, how to play a game, instruction leaflets, DIY books and so on.)

- Explain that they are going to write instructions to teach young spiders how to catch and kill a fly. Direct them to Chapter 5 to re-read where Charlotte explains to Wilbur how she does it.

- Based on Charlotte's explanation, invite the children to write a set of instructions incorporating appropriate features from the checklist developed with the class earlier. Encourage children to swap instructions to check the sequence, features and coherence of their instructions, especially the imperative verbs, sequence and purposeful title.

Differentiation

Support: Let the children complete interactive activity 'Sequencing instructions' to refresh their skills.

Extension: Ask the children to write a formal set of instructions on how to write good instructions, focusing on a helpful layout.

2. Wilbur's web

Objective

To rewrite narrative with Wilbur as narrator.

What you need

Copies of *Charlotte's Web*, printable page 'Storyboard (2)', interactive activity 'First or third?'.

What to do

- Discuss the difference between first- and third-person narrative. (Readers know things a character narrator would not know, versus being inside the thoughts of a character narrator, for example.)

- Ask: *Who narrates Charlotte's Web?* (Third person narrator.) *What tells you this?* (Pronouns, perspective from outside story.) *Do you prefer books in the first- or third-person?* Ask for examples. Boys may not enjoy books with a female narrator or vice versa.

- Ask: *How would* Charlotte's Web *change if Wilbur told the story? What wouldn't he know?* Bring the discussion round to the different knowledge and perspective of a character narrator. Wilbur could not know, for example, that Mrs Arable worried about Fern spending time with the animals. He also would not know what different characters were thinking unless they told him.

- Hand out printable page 'Storyboard (2)'. Ask the children to plot key events on it while you re-read the final chapter, focusing on what Wilbur would or would not know if he was telling the story.

- Using their storyboard as a plan, ask the children to rewrite the final chapter (independently) as if they were Wilbur telling the story. Remind them to write in Wilbur's voice and to include his reflections, as well as a recount of events.

Differentiation

Support: Let the children work through interactive activity 'First or third?', helping them to recognise first- and third-person narratives.

Extension: Be rigorous about children improving their writing, checking beyond common errors for ways to enhance their writing, such as using figurative or idiomatic language.

3. Dear Diary

Objective

To write for real purposes using different writing conventions.

What you need

Copies of *Charlotte's Web*, notebooks, photocopiable page 41 'Diary checklist', printable pages 'Zlata's Diary', 'The Diary of a Young Girl', 'Diary of a Wimpy Kid', 'The Secret Diary of Adrian Mole Aged 13 $\frac{3}{4}$'.

Cross-curricular link

Art and design

What to do

- Discuss different types of diaries, building up an idea web on the board: desk diary, pocket diary, diary on computer, phone, tablet, school diary, personal diary, and so on. Do a survey on whether the class use or keep a diary of any kind.

- Find out if the children have read any published diaries appropriate to their age: historical (*The Diary of a Young Girl*, *Zlata's Diary*) or fictional (*The Diary of a Killer Cat*, *The Secret Diary of Adrian Mole Aged 13 $\frac{3}{4}$*, *Diary of a Wimpy Kid* series). Read some short extracts from the printable pages.

- Ask: *What do you notice about the different styles of writing?* (Serious, humorous, honest, factual, fanciful, reflective, personal.) *What are the common features?* (First person, past tense, chronological, time connectives, paragraphs, informal, colloquial, chatty, thoughts and feelings.)

- Read parts of Chapter 19 on Templeton's time at the Fair. Explain that they are going to pretend to be Templeton, writing an entry in his diary about his time at the Fair. They must use all they know of him to capture his voice.

- Hand out photocopiable page 41 'Diary checklist'. Give planning time before the children write a first draft. Ask for volunteers to read out their drafts for feedback and suggestions. Encourage the children to review and improve their work using the checklist.

4. It's all in the words

Objective

To change the narrative by adding an episode.

What you need

Copies of *Charlotte's Web*, media resource 'Announcement', photocopiable page 42 'A new episode', scissors.

What to do

- Read Chapter 19, 'The Egg Sac', from where Avery notices the blue tag on Uncle's pen until the words *'Attention, please!'* Ask: *Whereabouts in the plot does this extract appear?* (The climax.) *What happened next?* (Homer is asked to take Wilbur to the judges' booth for a special award.)

- Play the audio clip from media resource 'Announcement'. The announcement asks for the first prize winner to receive his prize but says nothing about Wilbur.

- Cut and hand out the slips from photocopiable page 42 'A new episode'. The text follows the announcement, with everyone looking upset and disappointed in Wilbur. (Charlotte realises Wilbur is not yet saved and that she needs to weave one more stupendous word into her web to save him for sure, but she needs Templeton's help.) Give the children time to read the text independently.

- Allow time for groups to discuss possibilities for a new plot episode. Write on the board: What powerful message could Charlotte weave?

- After writing their new episodes, have a 'Readathon' of first drafts before allowing children to review and edit their episodes.

Differentiation

Support: Suggest words the children could 'weave' and discuss their episode ideas to support their planning.

Extension: Challenge children to produce an extended episode, including dialogue and characterisation in line with the original novel. Encourage them to review their work intensively at word, sentence and paragraph level, as well as for humour and style.

5. Summarise the story

Objective

To summarise the plot.

What you need

Interactive activity 'What's the main point?', copies of *Charlotte's Web*, notebooks, printable page 'Self-assessment cards'.

What to do

- Explain that a summary includes only essential information, leaving out unnecessary detail.

- Demonstrate how to summarise a sentence. Write on the board: *Wilbur's new friend is a large, grey spider about the size of a two pence piece, with eight legs.* Underline the nouns (and articles) and the verb. Ask: *Is any extra detail needed to understand this?* (No.)

- Work through the interactive activity 'What's the main point?', asking the children to identify key words to summarise the sentences.

- Tell the children they are going to summarise *Charlotte's Web* in pairs. Together, decide on the key plot events to become their paragraphs. (Fern saves Wilbur and moves to the Zuckerman's barn; Wilbur makes friends with Charlotte the spider; Wilbur discovers he is going to die; Charlotte spins her words and Wilbur becomes famous; Wilbur wins a special prize at the County Fair; Wilbur carries Charlotte's egg sac home safely.)

- Explain that summaries must be in chronological order and usually in the present tense. Remind them to include sequencing linking words, both inside and across paragraphs (but not repeating 'and then' or 'next' too much). Allow time for each child to write three paragraphs.

- Once finished, hand out printable page 'Self-assessment cards' and allow them to make changes.

Differentiation

Extension: Pairs can edit each other's paragraphs to check for irrelevant detail or repetition, and that they form a coherent summary.

6. My review

Objective

To write a review to recommend a book, giving reasons for their choices.

What you need

Copies of *Charlotte's Web*, notebooks, photocopiable page 43 'My book review', interactive activity 'Contrasts'.

What to do

- Talk about the book to help the class pull together some of the issues across the whole book.

- Ask: *What genre of book is it?* (Fantasy.) *Do you think it could also be a modern fable?* (Yes, animal characters, lessons to be learned, for example on friendship.) *What themes did we encounter running through the book?* (Friendship, helping others, self-sacrifice, personal journey.)

- Ask: *Do the illustrations fit the story?* (Yes, many are also very humorous.) Ask the children to share their favourite illustration, with reasons, with a partner. Share your favourite with the class.

- Ask: *Is the novel serious or humorous, happy or sad?* (All. It uses humour to delight and to illustrate more serious themes; it has both happy and sad moments.) Solicit examples, such as Wilbur 'spinning' a web, looking terrific and radiant, or Charlotte dying without seeing her children. Focus on these contrasts in the book in more detail by working through interactive activity 'Contrasts', where the children categorise various scenes from the story.

- Hand out photocopiable page 43 'My book review' for the children to complete. Emphasise that you are looking for a thoughtful review that reflects their personal opinions and views.

Differentiation

Support: Pair children to plan their reviews or complete one together.

Extension: Invite the children to research the author and his other children's novels, and write an opinion on whether they would like to read them.

Diary checklist

● Use this checklist to assess your diary entry for Templeton's time at the County Fair.

Feature	Example or evidence	Yes/No
I wrote in the first person.		
I wrote mostly in the past tense.		
The events are in chronological order.		
I wrote in Templeton's voice.		
I used informal/colloquial/ emotive language.		
I included interesting detail to engage the reader.		
I used a variety of sentence types.		
I wrote in clear paragraphs.		
I used time connectives to link events and paragraphs.		
I used interesting vocabulary.		
I checked my spelling and grammar carefully.		

A new episode

● Cut out the cards.

✂

Charlotte's weary frame sagged when Wilbur's name was not called out for a prize. She could sense everyone turning towards Wilbur's pen looking upset and disappointed.

She gazed down at Wilbur who was snoozing with a peaceful, untroubled expression. 'I can't let him down,' she thought. Summoning her dwindling energy, she scrabbled down to where Templeton was lurking.

'Emergency, Templeton. All hands on deck!'

'Oh, emergency is it? No time to waste I suppose. Well I heard the announcement. It's all over. Wilbur's bacon after all. I've wasted enough time on that lost cause.'

'He's not a lost cause!' snapped Charlotte. 'I won't let you say that and I won't let Wilbur be bacon either. What I need from you, one last time, is a word, a final stupendous word! Templeton! I won't take no for an answer. Get cracking. Get me that word!'

Charlotte's weary frame sagged when Wilbur's name was not called out for a prize. She could sense everyone turning towards Wilbur's pen looking upset and disappointed.

She gazed down at Wilbur who was snoozing with a peaceful, untroubled expression. 'I can't let him down,' she thought. Summoning her dwindling energy, she scrabbled down to where Templeton was lurking.

'Emergency, Templeton. All hands on deck!'

'Oh, emergency is it? No time to waste I suppose. Well I heard the announcement. It's all over. Wilbur's bacon after all. I've wasted enough time on that lost cause.'

'He's not a lost cause!' snapped Charlotte. 'I won't let you say that and I won't let Wilbur be bacon either. What I need from you, one last time, is a word, a final stupendous word! Templeton! I won't take no for an answer. Get cracking. Get me that word!'

My book review

 Use this template to write a book review of *Charlotte's Web*. Copy each heading and complete it after reading the questions below each heading.

Title:

Author: **Illustrator:**

Genre
What type of book is it: adventure, fantasy, slice of life, detective, science fiction? Is it humorous or serious?

Setting
Where does the story take place? (Mention more than one setting if relevant.) When is the story set? Does it matter?

Characters
Who are the main characters? What are they like? Which one was your favourite? How did the author build up the characters? How important were the illustrations?

Plot
What was the main idea in the plot? What was the problem or complication? Did you enjoy the way it was resolved?

Ending
How did the story end? Did you find the ending satisfying? Did it leave you feeling happy, sad, thoughtful, or something else?

Themes
What were the main themes running through the book? Did you learn anything from them?

Writing style
How would you describe the author's style? Was it written in the first or third person? What was the atmosphere or mood of the book?

Reflections
Did you enjoy the book? Why? Was it easy or difficult to read and understand? Would you change anything about the story if you could? Why? Did you learn anything from reading the book? What? Who would you recommend the book to?

ASSESSMENT

1. Q & A

Objective

To understand what they read.

What you need

Dictionaries, copies of *Charlotte's Web*, notebooks, photocopiable page 47 'Q & A', interactive activity 'Multiple choice'.

What to do

- Recall the 'open' question words already covered ('who', 'what', 'why', 'where', 'when', 'how'). Check if the children remember the difference between questions requiring a right or wrong answer and those requiring an opinion or judgement.

- Draw their attention to the different types of questions used to test their knowledge in other subjects. Can they find or give examples?

- Recall the skim-scan-read-response approach to answering questions based on a text. First skim the text for clues about context, such as title, heading, pictures, names, and first and last sentence. Next, scan the text, paying attention to details and identifying unfamiliar words in context. Then, skim the questions. After this, read the text, closely noting relevant information. Finally, answer the questions, beginning with questions requiring a right or wrong answer. Remind children that they can always leave a difficult question to last.

- Provide the children with dictionaries and copies of *Charlotte's Web* Chapter 15, and ask them to work through the questions on photocopiable page 47.

- Assess their ability to complete the activity independently, demonstrating their comprehension.

Differentiation

Support: Ask children to complete interactive activity 'Multiple choice'. Skim, scan and read through the text and questions with the children. Highlight easier questions and guide the children to complete them first.

Extension: Limit the time to complete the activity and challenge them to come up with their own similar style comprehension questions on the text to give to a partner to answer.

2. Commas make sense

Objective

To use commas to clarify meaning or avoid ambiguity in writing.

What you need

Copies of *Charlotte's Web*, interactive activity 'Commas make sense'.

What to do

- Ask the children to skim through *Charlotte's Web* for examples of commas separating words or phrases in lists, marking direct speech, or showing a pause between clauses, phrases and adverbials.

- Remind them that commas help clarify meaning. Let them work in pairs or groups. Write an unpunctuated sentence on the board and ask them to clarify its meaning using commas. For example: 'Templeton enjoyed the remains of peanut butter sandwiches chocolate custard tart cheese crackers fruit salad custard ice cream cakes and sweets.' Discuss all possible options, such as: 'chocolate, custard, tart'; 'chocolate custard, tart'; chocolate, custard tart'; and so on.

- Check they understand that ambiguity means the presence of two or more meanings in a text. Provide examples, such as: 'Let's eat Wilbur' and 'Let's eat, Wilbur'; 'Wilbur wasn't killed mercifully' and 'Wilbur wasn't killed, mercifully'; 'Charlotte finds comfort in eating, her words and Wilbur' and 'Charlotte finds comfort in eating her words and Wilbur.' The children should sit in small groups and discuss the ambiguity in each sentence and how the comma alters its meaning. Challenge them to invent examples to share.

- Open interactive activity 'Commas make sense' and let the children demonstrate their ability to use the comma to change or clarify meaning.

Differentiation

Support: Talk through the first couple of examples on the interactive activity, using speech patterns to emphasise the change in meaning.

Extension: Ask children to make up their own sentences to demonstrate ambiguity.

3. Prepare and present

Objective

To explain and discuss understanding of what they have read.

What you need

Copies of *Charlotte's Web*, printable page 'Barn spider factfile', research material, speech cards, Extract 4 (optional).

What to do

- In small groups, ask the children to list animals appearing in the book and discuss factual information mentioned about them.

- Groups can report back to the class and share information. Discuss how the information can be classified: appearance, what they eat, habitat and other behavioural traits. Display printable page 'Barn spider factfile' to revise a suitable format.

- The children should choose one animal from the story to research and present to the class. The information should be divided into different sections, as discussed, accompanied by a picture or diagram.

- Discuss presentation skills. Recall how the characters spoke when giving a speech: re-read the speeches in Chapter 12 where Charlotte speaks to the farm animals, Chapter 20 where the loudspeaker talks about Wilbur, and Chapter 22 where Wilbur addresses Charlotte's children. Ask: *How would you describe the tone of these speeches?* Discuss levels of formality and explain that although a speech or presentation is formal, it is not necessary to be too formal.

- Remind them about using speech cards and key words as prompts (not to write out in full).

- Assess their ability to give a formal presentation with clarity and confidence.

Differentiation

Support: Ask the children to prepare presentations on barn spiders (like Charlotte) using information from the book, Extract 4 and the factfile.

4. Write to a friend

Objective

To identify audience and purpose in writing.

What you need

Copies of *Charlotte's Web*, media resource 'Thank-you letter'.

Cross-curricular link

PSHE

What to do

- Read the book's final paragraph. Discuss why Charlotte was in a class of her own. Ask: *What was she good at?* (Being a friend and writing.)

- Ask: *Have you ever received a letter, card or email from a friend? How does it make you feel? Why?* (When someone takes time to write to you, you feel special.)

- Ask the children to think about which character in the story might write a thank-you letter to show appreciation for something, for example, Charlotte to Wilbur, Wilbur to Charlotte or even Wilbur to Templeton.

- Encourage children to be specific. Instead of saying 'thank you for everything', mention specific things they are grateful for. They should think about what each character might be thankful for.

- Consider the language together. Explain that a thank-you letter is a personal but formal way of expressing yourself, so children should avoid slang and colloquial terms.

- Ask the children to plan a thank-you letter from one character to another. Use the media resource 'Thank-you letter' as a model to frame their writing.

- Remind children to follow the writing process: plan, draft, write, edit and proofread.

- Assess their ability to write for a specific audience and purpose, using appropriate language.

Differentiation

Extension: Encourage the children to write and send a thank-you letter to a real friend.

5. A day in the life of a pig

Objective

To use organisational and presentational devices to structure text.

What you need

Copies of *Charlotte's Web*, examples of timetables, schedules or planners, printable page 'Personal daily planner'.

Cross-curricular links

PSHE, mathematics

What to do

- Together, read Chapter 4 describing Wilbur's daily schedule. A schedule is a list or plan of intended events for a specific period. Ask: *What is the purpose of a schedule? Who needs one? Did Wilbur need one? Why did he make plans for each day?* (It gave him purpose.)

- A schedule or timetable is usually set out in a structured way. Look at examples such as bus or school timetables. Discuss other useful organisational features for timetables, such as headings, tables, highlighted words, key words, bullets and capitalisation.

- Recall how to record time. In *Charlotte's Web*, the time is written in various ways: 'Twelve o'clock', 'six-thirty', and 'eight to nine'. Ask if the children know other formats to record time, such as 12.00 or 1pm. (Many ways are acceptable.)

- Invite the children to draw up a schedule for Wilbur based on the one in Chapter 4, using relevant organisational devices to structure the timetable and guide the reader.

- Assess their ability to organise, summarise and present the information in a way that is clear and easy to read.

Differentiation

Support: Let children use printable page 'Personal daily planner' as a writing frame.
Extension: Encourage children to create a day in the life of Templeton, Fern or Lurvy), which requires more creativity.

6. It's a miracle!

Objective

To perform their own composition.

What you need

Copies of *Charlotte's Web*.

What to do

- Assign the children roles from Chapter 11: Lurvy, Mr and Mrs Zuckerman, the minister. Read the chapter together, encouraging the children to read their parts with expression, focusing on appropriate intonation, pace and volume.

- The story says 'the news spread all over the county.' Ask: *How does news spread?* (By word of mouth, newspapers, television, radio, social media – today not then.)

- Ask the children to imagine there's a reporter on the scene in the story. In groups of four or five, let them role play interviews with the characters, giving a personal account of 'the miracle'. Remind them to speak in the first person, past tense.

- Challenge the children to then write a short news report for radio or television. It should have a lead in with information on who, what, where and when, followed by two to three segments (paragraphs) detailing why and how. It should also include quotes from various characters.

- Remind them to use adverbials to link ideas between sentences and paragraphs. Once their report is ready, ask them to read it out as a news reporter would read the news on TV or radio.

- Assess their ability to maintain eye contact, use appropriate expression and tone, speak clearly, and limit body movements so as not to distract the audience.

Differentiation

Support: Provide the children with a writing frame and sentence starters for the report.
Extension: Let the children research their own 'miraculous' event to report on – past or present.

Q & A

● Answer these questions about Chapter 15 on a separate sheet of paper.

1. Read the first paragraph of *Charlotte's Web* Chapter 15, 'The Crickets'.
   a. Who sang the song of summer's ending?
   b. Was it a happy or sad song?
   c. What does 'monotonous' mean?
   d. Use it in a sentence of your own.

2. What did the song of the crickets mean to these characters?
   a. Fern
   b. The young geese
   c. Lurvy
   d. Charlotte

3. What does it mean to be 'the centre of attraction'?

4. Look up the word 'radiant' in a dictionary.
   a. What does it mean?
   b. Where did they find it?
   c. Was it easy for Wilbur to look radiant?
   d. Did he succeed? How?

5. Which three words below best describe Wilbur's 'mixed feelings' at this
   point in the story?

   worried   sad   confident   lonely   proud   humble

6. Which sentence shows that Charlotte trusted Wilbur?

7. This chapter foreshadows change.
   a. Describe the tone (or mood).
   b. Find a sentence to support your answer.

8. Based on what happens from this point, explain 'the cycle of life'
   as a theme in the story.

SCHOLASTIC

Available in this series:

9781407142203

9781407142197

9781407142241

9781407142227

9781407142234

9781407158754 **JAN 2016**

9781407142258 **JAN 2016**

9781407158778 **JAN 2016**

9781407142289 **JAN 2016**

9781407142319 **JAN 2016**

9781407142265 **MAY 2016**

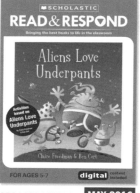

9781407142272 **MAY 2016**

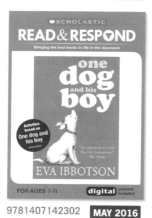

9781407142302 **MAY 2016**

9781407158761 **MAY 2016**

9781407158792 **MAY 2016**

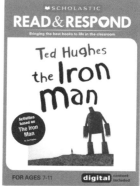

9781407142296 **MAY 2016**

To find out more, call: 0845 6039091
or visit our website www.scholastic.co.uk/readandrespond